A PLACE OF
BEAUTY

A 21-DAY DEVOTIONAL
FOR ARTISTS

EDITED BY CATHERINE MILLER

UNITED ADORATION

Dear Nancy & George,
God bless you in all the
ways you reflect His
creativity and encourage
artists. We're grateful
for you!
Blessings,
Nick & Kathryn

United Adoration is a ministry of Heartland Church.
1025 Vance Avenue, Fort Wayne, Indiana 46805

WWW.UNITEDADORATION.COM

978-1-7379278-0-8 (paperback)
978-1-7379278-1-5 (ebook)

CONTENTS

We need to exchange a static view of creation for a dynamic one. Creation is ongoing in the sense that God is involved in creation with his own two hands — incarnate Word and Spirit — embracing the world to bring it into its final destination, the new heavens and the new earth.

— ROBERT E. WEBBER, *The Divine Embrace*

Christians are called to enter into the chorus of praise that is true worship, responding in the Spirit to the revelation of the saving God in Jesus Christ. Theology is all about knowing how to sing the song of redemption; to know when to shout, when to mourn, when to be silent and when to hope. But in order to enjoy the song and sing it well, we must learn the words and the music.

— KELLY M. KAPIC, *A Little Book for New Theologians*

The Beauty of Healing

BY REV. DAVE FRINCKE

*To gather with God's people in united adoration of the Father
is as necessary to the Christian life as prayer.*

— MARTIN LUTHER

We held our first United Adoration Retreat in the fall of 2014. We didn't know what to expect from this three-day experiment. Our lack of expectation was fueled mostly by the fact that we didn't know what we were doing. We had never run a *retreat* before, and most of us in attendance had never even attended a collaborative, multi-day creative event like this. All we had to hold onto was a simple goal: We wanted to bring songwriters together to collaboratively write and record a collection of songs.

I remember being really nervous as attendees began showing up at a small church in Oak Park, Illinois. I only knew a few of the fifteen retreat attendees and was unsure how collaborating with strangers was going to go. I had no idea that the next three days were going to change my life forever.

Our simple goal for the retreat was met. This group of strangers wrote a bunch of songs together and even produced a recording project. But that's not the real story of the retreat.

Throughout our three days together, God was giving us glimpses into each other's lives. As we ate together, prayed together, took walks together, and collaborated in every nook and cranny of the church, people began to share their struggles. Some of the artists felt spiritually empty. Other artists were in the midst of transition and were unsure of the future. Some artists were in the middle of ugly church infighting. Some were in conflict with their pastors. And almost everyone was dealing with feelings of rejection.

This vulnerability created opportunities for all of us to pray for one another, encourage one another, and engage in powerful times of ministry. In light of how the Holy Spirit was moving, the songwriting became secondary. The songs we wrote are good, but the people who wrote them are precious.

That first retreat completely changed the mission of United Adoration. What we experienced excited us but also opened our eyes to the realities that so many artists live with while serving in their local church. We knew that we couldn't just be another arts movement; we had to be a healing movement as well.

ARTISTS AND THE CHURCH

I am in my twentieth year of ministry and currently in my sixth year of serving as the rector (or senior pastor, depending on your tradition) of Heartland Church in Fort Wayne, Indiana. Before that, I served as a worship leader for fifteen years. I've experienced the struggles of serving as a church musician and the struggles of serving as a pastor. I've been on the giving and receiving side of the disconnect that is common between pastors and artists. I've seen the destruction that dissonance between artists and the local church can bring. And I've seen the power that comes when artists and their church are in harmony.

Even after twenty years, I can authentically say this: I love artists, I love pastors, and I love the Church. Artists and pastors each have a unique assignment that prepares the Church to accomplish her mission.

This is one of the values that drives us at United Adoration: We believe that artists are essential to the mission of the Church. Artists have a call to declare the awe and wonder of God to the world through what they create. They have a God-given creativity to take the truth of God — his Word, his character, and his gospel — and deliver it in a way that penetrates our souls. If artists are feeling rejected by their local congregations and disconnected from their pastors, their faith begins to struggle, and the mission of the Church suffers.

At United Adoration, we are on a mission to revitalize the creativity of the local church by empowering artists to create in their own language, culture, and context. We have a core set of convictions that move us forward in our mission.

1. We believe that God wants artists to be received, cared for, and appreciated by their pastors and churches.
2. We believe that God wants artists of all disciplines to create art that glorifies God, ministers to people in their home churches, and shares the wonder and beauty of God with the world.
3. We believe that God wants artists and pastors to work together to create healthy creative communities within local churches.

These convictions are helping to foster greater collaboration among artists, pastors, churches, cities, and movements. As this kind of culture is established in local churches, an explosion of creativity happens which results in the Church engaging our world with the gospel of Jesus Christ in fresh ways.

A PLACE OF BEAUTY

This collection of devotions was compiled with these convictions in mind. They were written by artists and pastors to speak directly to the issues that artists face. Don't let this be a devotional that you just skim over. Be sensitive to how God is speaking to you through it. What does God want you to learn? How is he encouraging you? Which of your thought patterns is he wanting to correct? What is he leading you to step out and create?

Each day includes a reflection on a theme or Scripture passage, suggestions for further Old and New Testament readings to connect that day's theme to the broader biblical story, and a spiritual practice to extend your time with God. Allow the closing prayer each day to lead you into an extended time of waiting, listening, journaling, and worship.

As a pastor, let me say this to every artist reading this book: Pastors need you and the Church needs you. We receive your creative spirit and want to see you flourish in the Church. As you grow in your faith and relationship with God, we all benefit. As you move forward in your journey with God and create along the way, we get to see a bit more of His wonder. Together, we can create a place of beauty.

God's Beautiful Images, Engraved on Our Hearts

BY REV. JACK KING

I am the good shepherd. I know my own and my own know me...

— JOHN 10:14

I have a file in my office that I call "the treasure of the parish." It's a file containing the spiritual autobiographies written by our people when they joined the parish as new members. I keep these files safe and secure, remembering that several have entrusted difficult parts of their spiritual stories to me in confidence. I read with awe of the powerful, redemptive work of Christ in people's lives. I see the beauty of God when I hear the hunger for God and the longing for authentic, spiritual community. As a rector, who a person *is*, hidden and redeemed in Christ, matters so much more to me than what a person might *do* for Christ or our parish. In these stories I find the beauty of God in the depths of someone's soul.

Another treasure of our parish is the parish pictorial directory. I know pictorial directories are falling out of fashion in an age of Facebook, Twitter, and Instagram profiles. As for me and my parish, we'll keep the parish pictorial directory updated. Faces are expressions of the soul, an

1

outward, visible depiction of the image of God within a human being.

I use the pictorial directory as a tool for prayer — maybe intercessory prayer, but usually prayers of thanksgiving. To pause over a person or a family's image, I give thanks for *who* they are in Christ. I want to perceive who people are in Christ. I can't do that if I only see them as potential volunteers for a ministry need. The people God has entrusted to my care are bearers of the beauty of God. If I don't see that — if I don't *desire* to see God's beauty within those entrusted to my care — I'll reduce the mystery of human beings to the functions they perform. These relationships are gifts. That's the heritage we have from the earliest pages of the Bible.

If you ever wonder about the place of beauty in Scripture, just go back to the tabernacle and the temple. The portions of Exodus concerning the tabernacle are the selections in a daily lectionary or Bible-reading plan that one is tempted to skim or skip altogether. Lots of materials and measurements, names of tribes and clans. What importance could they have?

Tremendous importance, actually. Especially if you're seeking the beauty of God among his people. In Exodus 28, God commands all skilled craftsmen to construct a breastplate that Aaron will wear as Israel's high priest in the Holy of Holies. If you ever doubt God's affection for artists, just remember how God enlisted artists to make the structures, fixtures, and garments "for glory and for beauty" in his tabernacle (Exodus 28:2, Exodus 35:30–36:7).

Aaron bore the names of Israel's twelve tribes on his breastplate. The names were not stitched onto this garment. God commanded that the names of Israel's twelve tribes be engraved on *precious stones*, affixed to the breastplate, in a grid of four rows, three stones for each row. Gold, onyx, topaz, emerald, sapphire, diamonds — the most beautiful stones in creation were selected to represent the tribes of God's people.

Interestingly, these same gems appear in the fixtures of Solomon's temple as well. They reappear in the throne room of Revelation, too. It's a sign that God's people, his treasured possession, are destined to become "living stones" in his Temple (1 Peter 2:5).

But from the beginning, we remember these names as bearers of God's image and beauty. Names engraved on precious stones were fixed to Aaron's heart. The physicality of that breastplate conveyed to Aaron that God's people are his treasured possession (see Exodus 19:5). As God treasures his people, so must his priests.

As a priest, I go back to the tabernacle, both in Scripture and in my heart, to renew my calling as a shepherd of Christ's flock. God requires that we approach his holy presence with his people on our hearts. Our Lord Jesus exemplified this loving care when he spoke about his vocation as the Good Shepherd: "When he has brought out all his own, he goes before them, and the sheep follow him, for they know his voice" (John 10:4). Certainly that is an image of pastoral care, yet it is also an important image for all who lead God's people in worship.

Pastors and musicians serve together in worship, sharing this holy and awe-filled calling to lead God's people to the throne of grace. The work of leading worship — all the planning, writing, rehearsing, singing, preaching — will be empty unless we love the Lord's people as we have been loved. That means loving people first for who they *are*, not for what tasks they *do*.

I once heard a friend share an experience from a retreat that Michael Card led for Christian musicians. The most memorable counsel Card offered to his fellow artists was, "You are not your gift." I try to hold that wise counsel before my heart as a preacher. It helps me to remember that love is the first and highest calling in my vocation. More than any gift I might have, love is the virtue I need most in order to be the Lord's servant in worship.

Yes, God has entrusted us with his gifts. But the depth and mystery of a person is not synonymous with those gifts. The depth and mystery of a fellow believer can only be comprehended in Paul's words, "your life is hidden with Christ in God" (Colossians 3:3). Lean into that mystery with those in your parish and you will see them anew. And it just may transform the way you experience worship with God's people on Sunday mornings, too.

Meditate further: Exodus 28; 1 Peter 2:4–10

APPLICATION

Take your parish directory and begin using it as a tool for prayer. Look at the faces in the photos in an unhurried manner. Pray a simple sentence prayer of thanksgiving over each photo, such as, "Heavenly Father, I give you thanks for N. and the ways [he/she/they] reveal your image and goodness in our parish."

You may come across the face of someone who is difficult for you — perhaps someone who has been a source of present or past conflicts. With Philippians 4:8 as your guide, offer a prayer of thanksgiving for this person.

PRAYER

> Heavenly Father, Maker of heaven and earth, you have given the splendor of your holy image to all human beings. Grant that we may see the goodness of your image in all persons, and especially among those in our parish. Guide the eyes of our hearts to perceive our brothers and sisters' lives "hidden with Christ in God" (Colossians 3:3), giving thanks always and everywhere for the many ways you reveal divine beauty through your people. Through Jesus Christ our Lord, who lives and reigns with you and the Holy Spirit, one God, for ever and ever.
>
> *Amen*

Imagination and the Nature of God

BY CATHERINE MILLER

All creatures look to you to give them their food at the proper time.
When you give it to them, they gather it up; when you open your hand,
they are satisfied with good things.

— PSALM 104:27-28

My view of God changed dynamically when I began to connect with the Creator as an artist. Until a few years ago, I never saw myself in the stories of the Bible, although I longed to be like the brave heroine Esther. I didn't know about the artist Bezalel (Exodus 31) or Chenaniah, the Levite who oversaw the musicians (1 Chronicles 15:22). Seeing the wonder of the world as the canvas of a Master Artist has helped me find myself in God's grand story. He painted the skies with the stars, shaped the planets, poured the oceans, breathed life into the birds. With creativity and color, he made hummingbirds that flap their wings at fifty-three beats per second and designed the abdomen of the venomous peacock spider in shades of iridescent blue and red. With humor and imagination, he made the sea monster, Leviathan, to play with (Psalm 104:26). God creates *for his own pleasure.*

I almost gave up being a musician a few years ago. I remember thinking, *If I can't make money as a pianist, songwriter or writer, what's the point? Does anybody care about my music? Why bother trying?* As a stay-at-home mom, I was struggling to make money in my chosen profession. I remember sitting at home one day, crying. *Is this what my life is going to be like? Why did I bother going to music school?* My day was filled with changing poopy diapers and folding mountains of laundry, and the sudden change from work to home left me feeling alone and overwhelmed. I was depressed. My self-worth was wrapped up in my external works and vocation.

But as my children have grown, my eyes have been opened to view the world through their eyes. As they express their curiosity and cherish the horseshoe crab, the cardinal, and the sunflower, I find that the fragrant smell of jasmine on my back porch or a moonlit walk on a hot summer night offer glimpses of the Artist. If God created a sea monster for sheer joy and pleasure, how might that translate to my artistry as a mother? Might I, too, create simply because I take pleasure in *making*?

My work as an artist is an act of worship. I can play piano, sing, and write songs and essays because it brings me joy and blesses the people around me. Time spent connecting to God enriches my creativity and nurtures my soul, making me a better mother. *This is who I am.* I am an artist, a mother, and a child of God. I don't have to choose. Horatius Bonar's hymn, "Not What My Hands Have Done" (1864) speaks to this. He says that our works cannot bring us salvation or peace with God; we must dwell on his work and his grace alone. The final verse says:

> I praise the God of grace;
> I trust his truth and might;
> he calls me his, I call him mine,
> my God, my joy, my light.
> 'Tis he who saveth me,

and freely pardon gives;
I love because he loveth me,
I live because he lives.

Our work as artists connects us to a Creator whose works are beautiful and precious to him. We nurture our souls when we spend time in God's Word, learning who he is; when we create, reflecting his glory; and when we bask in nature, inspired by the wondrous diversity of God's creation.

Meditate further: Exodus 31; Hebrews 9

APPLICATION

Reading Scripture provides two benefits of particular interest to you as an artist: It renews your mind with truth, and it expands your vision of who God is and who he created you to be. Memorizing passages of the Bible gives you the ability to recall, at will, these truths. This is critical in your daily spiritual battle for joy and peace in Christ.

To begin memorizing Scripture, start with this exercise:

1. Pick a single verse. For example, Psalm 103:1 — "Bless the LORD, O my soul, and all that is within me, bless his holy name!"

2. Say the verse out loud.

3. Say it again, but this time try placing emphasis on a few words. For example: "**Bless** the LORD, O **my** soul, and **all** that is within me, **bless** his holy name!"

4. Say it a third time, emphasizing different words: "Bless the **LORD**, O my **soul**, and all that is within **me**, bless **his** holy name!"

5. Now write down the verse as you speak it.

PRAYER

From the song "O Great Physician" by Catherine and Henry Miller

Creator God, create in me
A soul that yearns for you
Creator God, create in me
A mind that loves your truth

Creator God, create in me
A heart that sings your praise
Creator God, create in me
A will that walks your ways

Amen

Distinguished by His Presence

BY KATHRYN KIRCHER

And [Moses] said to him, "If your presence will not go with me, do not bring
us up from here. . . . Is it not in your going with us, so that we are distinct,
I and your people, from every other people on the face of the earth?"

— EXODUS 33:15-16

As artists who are also Jesus followers, what is it that distinguishes us from other creatives? Certainly we are set apart by our motives: In our artistry we strive for more than self-expression and personal benefit, creating also to honor God and edify his people. We are also differentiated by the content of our art: Even if the subject of our work is not overtly religious, the product is always affected by the values of our faith.

Perhaps what sets us apart most as Jesus-following creatives is that we carry his presence with us. As they traveled through the wilderness, the people of Israel had a cloud by day and fire by night to show that God was with them. We have something infinitely more precious, even if it is not as showy as a pillar of fire. God's very own Spirit dwells inside of us — a privilege that the wandering Israelites never had.

His "going with us" sets us apart — especially as we create. The breath of the same Holy Spirit that hovered over the chaos at Creation continues to hover over our lives and inspire us as we ply our arts. The Spirit's presence is inherent even in the etymology of the word "inspire." It comes from the Latin words *in* and *spirare* — "to breathe," related to *spiritus*, "breath" or "spirit." We are inspired when the Holy Spirit breathes in us. Historically, "inspire" carried the connotation of being influenced or guided by the power of the Holy Spirit.

That same Holy Spirit breathes on you and me today as we seek to create works of art that honor the Lord, express his kingdom, and touch the hearts of those around us. Just as the Israelites were distinct from the surrounding peoples because of God's presence, we are distinguished by his presence with us and in us, inspiring us as we create. As we practice our various art forms, let us consciously invite his presence into our process, that our works may be truly inspired by that holy breath of heaven.

Meditate further: Exodus 19; Hebrews 10

APPLICATION

The traditional greeting of the Maori people of New Zealand, the *hongi*, is performed by pressing noses and foreheads together and sharing a breath. The next time you begin a creative work, make it a point to invite the Holy Spirit to breathe into you. You might even want to use your holy imagination to picture sharing a *hongi* with the Lord as you welcome Him.

PRAYER

Come, Holy Spirit. Fill my mind, heart, and will with your creative breath. Let me be an instrument in your hands to create a taste of the new creation that is yet to come. Show me what you want to create through me.

Amen

Made in Your Image

BY HENRY MILLER

There is one body and one Spirit, just as you were called to one hope
when you were called; one Lord, one faith, one baptism;
one God and Father of all, who is over all and through all and in all.

— EPHESIANS 4:4-6, NIV

After God created people, he surveyed everything that he had made and said it was very good. The word we translate as "good," *tov*, isn't just like telling somebody "good job" or "that meal was really good." It's a word that connotes beauty, satisfaction, and harmony. That's the kind of world that we are created for, and that's the kind of people that we are created to be. God designed us to rest in his peace, in his *shalom*. But of course, the world today is not all *tov*, and we do not always experience *shalom*.

The hymn "You Made Us in Your Image," by Kate Bluett (and set to music by Catherine Miller), was created as a response to the injustices that seemed to come from every side in 2020. In Isaiah 58, God contrasts an outwardly religious but inwardly empty type of fast with what he describes as the fast he chooses (Isaiah 58:6, 7) — to free the oppressed, to cast off the yoke of bondage, and to feed the hungry. The church of God is the largest, most diverse, most creative, and most healing group of people anywhere in history, anywhere in the world. It's easy for us to think about church and only think of the faces of the people that we see on a Sunday.

We must remember that we have brothers and sisters in every nation, every city, from every imaginable background, culture, or ethnicity, and yet we are unified in our worship of the triune God. If you've ever had the privilege of worshiping God with Christians who come from a different nation or speak a different language or who look quite different from you, then you have seen a glimpse of heaven. When the mosaic of God's people is finally revealed in all its fullness, we will glorify God as the people who are made in his image from across time and space. Just as you had a part to play in the body of your local church, the church in your city or your country has its own part to play to fully bring about the design of what God has in mind for his new creation.

Meditate further: Isaiah 58; Revelation 21

APPLICATION

Find a friend who speaks a different language or grew up in a different tribe, region, or country from you. Ask this friend to share a favorite song from his or her home church with you.

PRAYER

The Prayer for Social Justice from The Book of Common Prayer *(2019)*

> Almighty God, you created us in your own image. Grant us grace to contend fearlessly against evil and to make no peace with oppression, and help us to use our freedom rightly in the establishment of justice in our communities and among the nations, to the glory of your holy Name; through Jesus Christ

our Lord, who lives and reigns with you and the Holy Spirit, one God, now and forever.

Amen

YOU MADE US IN YOUR IMAGE

by Kate Bluett

Almighty God, you made us in your image
Each one of us is born to show your face
As Triune God, you suffer no division,
Unite us by your all-suffusing grace.

Give fearlessness when we contend with evil;
Let us refuse to give oppression peace.
You give us, Lord, the freedom of your people;
Give courage, too, 'til all oppression cease.

Oh, let us use the gifts you give us rightly
For justice in our homes and in our lands
Until the glory of your name shines brightly,
And not a stone of death's dominion stands.

All praise the Father, all who bear God's image,
And praise the ever living, loving Son,
All praise the Spirit, guiding still our mission
To live and love 'til all may live as one.

Ex Nihilo

BY KATHRYN KIRCHER

In the beginning, God created the heavens and the earth.
The earth was without form and void, and darkness was over the face of the deep.
And the Spirit of God was hovering over the face of the waters.

— GENESIS 1:1-2

When I think about Jesus' coming to earth, I'm struck by the fact that our Messiah basically came to us out of nothing. Of course, he existed with God before the foundation of the world, but when he arrived here on earth, he was born from the womb of a virgin. Impossible! There was emptiness there. Only an egg — no sperm. That isn't how babies are made.

Ex nihilo is an adverb (Latin) meaning "out of nothing." Isn't that like God? Repeatedly throughout history, he has delighted in coming to us and making himself known through times of emptiness, barrenness, and impossibility. Creating *ex nihilo* is an expression of his character and nature. Some examples:

- The creation of the heavens and the earth out of what was dark, void, and without form (Genesis 1)
- The provision of manna, the food of angels, for forty years in

the wilderness; it just appeared out of nowhere like the dew (Exodus 16)

- The flesh that covered the dry bones and the breath that came into those rattling skeletons — life emerged where there was nothing but death (Ezekiel 37)

- The flour and the oil that continued to pour out of almost-empty vessels for two destitute widows (1 Kings 17 and 2 Kings 4)

- The tax payments that came from the mouth of a fish (Matthew 17)

- The miracles that Jesus and his disciples performed — sight and hearing where there was none, health out of sickness, robust limbs out of what was lame, life out of death, strength out of weakness, well-muscled hands out of what was withered, soundness of mind out of demonic madness (the Gospels and Acts).

Papa God loves to bring something out of nothing. Every place there is lack, weakness, emptiness, impossibility, sickness, hopelessness, or barrenness is a place where his propensity for creating *ex nihilo* can shine.

This is the same God whose Holy Spirit dwells in us. When we create, we don't have God's capacity to produce something *ex nihilo*, but we reflect the creativity of his character as his image-bearers. When we choreograph an original dance, write a poem, paint a portrait, or pen the lyrics to a new melody, we birth something that has never existed before — a new work that can speak to the emptiness and hopelessness in the world with Spirit-led creativity.

The privilege we have as artists is to echo God's creativity and release our handiwork into places of emptiness and lack, barrenness and impossibility. As we continue to create in partnership with God's

Holy Spirit, let's fix our hearts on the One who specializes in bringing something out of nothing.

Meditate further: Genesis 1; John 1

APPLICATION

When you pray, invite the Holy Spirit into your time of creativity. Take note of the images, words, and people who come to your mind. Let your relationship with God inspire your creativity.

PRAYER

A collect based on Psalm 104 by Catherine Miller

> Divine Artist, you are clothed with splendor and majesty. In wisdom you filled the earth with beauty and life. Bring inspiration and direction to my work as an artist, O God; guide my hands, my lips, my mind, so that my work brings honor to you, bringing life to the world around me.
>
> *Amen*

A Feast in the Wasteland

BY KATHRYN KIRCHER

Can God spread a table in the wilderness?

— PSALM 78:19

"Can God spread a table in the wilderness?" When the children of Israel asked this question, they were speaking against God, voicing a spirit of rebellion — yet in the abstract, these words raise a realistic question. How *could* God prepare a feast in the middle of the wilderness? Ingredients were limited in that bleak wasteland. It was an empty, barren desert.

I might have been tempted to ask this question when my husband and I visited Craters of the Moon National Monument in Idaho. The site was the scene of a volcanic eruption about 2,000 years ago, and its desolations reminded me of Israel's wilderness journey. Those ancient lava flows created vast, barren areas where nothing seems to grow for miles and miles. Massive fields of rich, black soil sprawl across the landscape, looking as though they have just been tilled, except these fields were "tilled" two millennia ago, and those huge clumps of soil are actually black basalt rocks. These are the least fertile fields you could ever find! Two thousand years after that cataclysmic volcanic activity, death still appears to reign in that bleak landscape . . . until you take a closer look.

We were stunned as we hiked through this area and began to see how much wildlife was actually living there. It is amazing to see the things that are able to grow — and even thrive! — in this desolate setting.

We learned that life there starts with the lichens. These organisms may be one of the simplest life forms on earth, but they have the amazing ability to grow on rocks where nothing else can grow. Patches of bright green, soft white, and deep rust embellished ancient boulders with color. Once those lichens are established, they set off a chain of life that starts encroaching on the barren black fields of the Craters of the Moon.

There are cinder gardens where clumps of flowers grow out of the heaps of fine black volcanic grit. Rabbitbrush, cushion buckwheat, and eight (!) different varieties of sagebrush have all somehow gained a foothold in this inhospitable environment. As the afternoon sun beat down, we even spotted a smoothstem blazingstar that was beginning to unfold its delicate yellow blossoms, even though it normally would not open until dusk.

In some areas, a hardy conifer called limber pine has been able to find enough nutrition in the volcanic soil to set down roots and begin to grow. And the birds! Anyone who knows me knows that I love birds! We saw rock wrens and turkey vultures, magpies and kestrels, rock pigeons and ravens. There was even a new one for me: Clark's nutcracker.

We were utterly fascinated to see how such a hostile environment could yield an exceedingly rich variety of plants and animals. This place at first glance seemed completely unable to sustain life, but it was actually bursting with beauty and vitality. It spoke to us deeply about God's ability to take the most barren, inhospitable places and bring forth life.

And that is just as true in our lives as it is in nature.

Sometimes there is a dry, broken place in our hearts where hopelessness seems to be the only thing growing. At other times there is a barren wasteland in our creativity: We want — or need — to produce something, but we are dry and empty, as if a drought has overtaken the garden of our creativity and sucked all the life out.

Yet somehow, as Father God breathes on us, life and creativity will begin to emerge once again. Dead seeds will sprout. Life and ingenuity can gain a foothold once more. Strength and innovation will return. Barren branches are able to sprout, and vision blossoms once again. Fruit can be borne in places that once seemed too desolate to be revived. The prophet Isaiah expressed God's unique, life-bringing capacity like this:

> I will turn deserts into lakes.
> I will turn dry land into springs.
> I will plant cedar, acacia, myrtle, and wild olive trees in the desert.
> I will place cedar, fir, and cypress trees together in the wilderness.
> People will see and know.
> Together they will consider and understand
> that the LORD's power has done this,
> that the Holy One of Israel has created it.
> — Isaiah 41:18b–20, GW

I guess God really *is* able to "spread a table in the wilderness"! May he breathe on the bleak desert places in your life and mine, once again performing the resurrection miracle that brings life and fruitfulness out of barrenness, drought, and loss.

Meditate further: Exodus 16; Revelation 19:1–10

APPLICATION

The beauty of nature is a balm to the human soul. Take a walk outside in your neighborhood, or visit a park or garden. Bring a journal with you.

Listen to the sounds of the garden: What captures your imagination? Write down the words and images that inspire you.

PRAYER

Divine Healer, you are the living water. Heal the brokenness in my soul, and bring life to the desert of my pain, strength to my weakness, innovation to my creative drought. Stir in me a desire to know you more, so that my life may bear fruit in desert wastelands.

Amen

Be Still and Move Forward

BY ELISE MASSA

Then the Lord said to Moses, "Why do you cry to me?
Tell the people of Israel to go forward."

— EXODUS 14:15

Choosing salad dressing can be stressful. I had spent six months overseas in New Zealand living on a compound. I vaguely remembered having maybe one or two choices for salad dressing at our communal dinners. Now, back in the United States, I stood before a vast wall of Kraft, Newman's Own, and generic brands. All the options seemed to flow as far as the hills of Hidden Valley! I found myself paralyzed by the sheer number of choices at my fingertips. Yes, choosing salad dressing can be stressful.

Years later, I felt paralyzed again when facing only two choices. I had spent ten years working as a bivocational minister to artists. I currently held a full-time position at a university, sneaking away to compose songs in the wee hours of the morning. Now, my heart was being drawn toward immersing myself fully in the artistic work and mission. The Lord's voice was not the only voice that I was hearing. I had a cacophony of voices inside my head offering advice. My parents' wisdom urged the practical and tangible. Our finite finances elicited caution. Even the beauty of the art world teemed with weeds, threatening to choke my unique voice and swallow me into the dirt of failed endeavors. How could I discern the Lord's voice among so many?

Moses heard a similar cacophony arise from the Israelites at the Red Sea. Immediately following their deliverance from slavery, they stood on a shoreline of impassible waters, with a vengeful despot and army in hot pursuit. The Israelites' screams, insults, doubts, and desperation rose and roared like the waves of the sea. When I imagine this situation, I picture Moses doing what any parent does when looking for an exit ramp and driving a van of complaining children: he turns down the radio and commands them to be quiet: "The LORD will fight for you, and you have only to be silent" (Exodus 14:14). Faced with impossible odds — Pharaoh would kill them, the sea would swallow them — Moses called the people to stillness. I imagine the hush of the people, with tight chests and bated breath. How could silence help at a time like this?

The Lord often imparts miracles at impasses, if we would but "be still, and know" that he is God. Through the silence, the Lord speaks, "Why do you cry to me? Tell the people of Israel to go forward." In the stillness of his people, the Lord confirmed the direction they were heading and the risk that it involved. Where was forward? Through the sea. Like the camp song, they couldn't go under it! Couldn't go around it! They had to go *through* it. *What are you waiting for*, the Lord seemed to say. *Go! Move!* And as Moses lifted the staff, the Lord that hovered over the waters now stood the waters on end, revealing the promised off ramp into the promised land.

In *Naming the Animals*, Stephen Roach writes, "Whatever step you take toward the creative partnership with God — be it large or small — *take it.* This is your next step, and this is a way to enrich the community and bring glory to God." What impasse stands between you and a holy endeavor? Whatever the risk, take heart. The Lord has designed you to express his beauty and hope into this world in the unique ways that he uniquely made you.

So — what are you waiting for? Be still and move forward.

Meditate further: Isaiah 41; Hebrews 11

APPLICATION

The cacophony of internal and external voices is real. We are barraged with curated images of success and cringing scenes of failure. There are false prophets promising instant glory and false teachers imposing unrealistic frameworks. Only in stillness can we practice discerning the Lord's voice among the legions. Set aside ten minutes. For the first two minutes, speak, list, or journal to the Lord about your fears, your hopes, and your questions. Then, take eight minutes of silence and invite the Lord to respond. Listen for unexpected phrases, images, or Scripture that might arise in your heart or mind. Then, find time to talk to a trusted mentor or friend about this experience, inviting this person to share his or her own thoughts and confirm or sharpen what you might have heard from the Lord.

PRAYER

Collect for Purity from The Book of Common Prayer *(2019)*

> Almighty God, to you all hearts are open, all desires known, and from you no secrets are hidden. Cleanse the thoughts of our hearts by the inspiration of your Holy Spirit, that we may perfectly love you and worthily magnify your holy Name. Through Christ our Lord,
>
> *Amen*

From Loneliness
to Solitude

BY CATHERINE MILLER

How long, O Lord? Will you forget me forever?
How long will you hide your face from me?

— PSALM 13:1

I have struggled with loneliness throughout my life. For a long time, I tried to fill my loneliness with television, projects, and relationships. I abhorred silence. In the words of Henri Nouwen,

> When we feel lonely, we keep looking for a person or persons who can take our loneliness away. Our lonely hearts cry out, 'Please hold me, touch me, speak to me, pay attention to me.' But soon we discover that the person we expect to take our loneliness away cannot give us what we ask for" (*Bread for the Journey: A Daybook of Wisdom and Faith*, 19).

During the pandemic, I found myself cut off from routines and interactions I had grown to depend on for my self-worth and identity.

Ironically, this disruption of routine laid the groundwork for me to have a closer relationship with God and develop healthy community.

As the pandemic forced United Adoration members to adjust plans for in-person retreats around the world, they began experimenting with online creative sessions and song shares. These online events gave me an opportunity to connect with other artists at a time when I was isolated. One of the women I met made it a point to speak truth and life to me through words of encouragement. The Spirit-filled prayer I experienced in these relationships pushed me into a season of creativity and collaboration that helped me heal from the negative self-image I had been clinging to.

The feelings of loneliness I had carried for so long were rooted in this negative self-image. I kept looking to other people to fulfill my need to be loved and understood. As I healed, I came to realize that *I am already the beloved.* As Henri Nouwen says,

> Who am I? I am the beloved. That's the voice Jesus heard when he came out of the Jordan River: "You are my beloved; on you my favor rests." And Jesus says to you and to me that we are loved as he is loved ("Moving from solitude to community to ministry," *Leadership*, Spring 1995, 81–87).

God was gently teaching me to seek my peace and rest in him and to stop expecting other people to provide it. He was changing my fear of loneliness into an embrace of solitude. In solitude, I sat with God. I cried, and he comforted me. The Psalms gave me a language to speak to God in my loneliness. I lamented:

> If you heal the broken pieces of my soul
> Who would I become? Where might I go?
> If you lead me to the water, will I run?
> Will I hide my face? Or will I follow?

My path from loneliness to solitude was paved with Spirit-filled community, encouragement, and creativity. Establishing healthy relational and spiritual rhythms helped me to rest in knowing that I am loved by the God of love, and from that rest I can reach out to and love others.

Meditate further: Hosea 2:14–23; Mark 5:21–43

APPLICATION

Take a moment each day to stop what you are doing and remember that God is with you, that you are his beloved, and that you are made for union with him. A helpful tool for this practice is the One Minute Pause app by John Eldredge, which is free to download to your smartphone.

PRAYER

Meditate on Psalm 91:1–2. *Come, Holy Spirit.*

> He who dwells in the shelter of the Most High
> will abide in the shadow of the Almighty.
> I will say to the LORD, "My refuge and my fortress,
> my God, in whom I trust."

Amen

Comparison

BY CATHERINE MILLER

But if you have bitter jealousy and selfish ambition in your hearts,
do not boast and be false to the truth. This is not the wisdom that comes
down from above, but is earthly, unspiritual, demonic.

— JAMES 3:13–15

I almost stopped being a musician several years ago. I had no record, no money, no piano, and nobody to collaborate with or listen to my music except for my husband. I began to think, *What's the point? Maybe I need to take a hard look at myself and admit that I'm just not that good.* Comparing my situation to others' led me to jealousy, bitterness, anger, and rage. I became depressed without music in my life, and I grew bitter toward my young children and jealous of people I believed to be successful.

The root cause of my issues, though, was my own insecurity. I was afraid that if I wasn't measuring up to the world's standards and the perceived expectations of others, I couldn't be loved. I was centering my value as an artist on worldly measures: products created, money earned, and even how many people were interested in using my music. When our metric of our self-worth is what others say about us, instead of what God says about us, we are poised to lose our identity to the whim of the moment.

At the end of a songwriting retreat, my husband pulled Rachel Wilhelm aside and insisted she listen to a song that we had written before she drove home. After I finished singing, she complimented the wide melody and the lyrics and asked, Why haven't you shared this with your church? Her encouragement breathed life into my soul and began the work of unshackling me from my expectations. I was like Eustace in C. S. Lewis's *Voyage of the Dawn Treader* transforming from his dragon state: I couldn't remove the scales of pain, woundedness, and comparison on my own. Encouragement came as an external breath of the Holy Spirit, removing layers of protection I had placed around my heart.

As Rachel's words pierced my heart, I felt my heart soften. I could see my calling: to create with God, in submission to his will. God had blessed me with musical craftsmanship so I could participate in his work of building on the church.

On the United Adoration website, it says:

> For many local artists serving inside their own local communities, there is a crisis of identity. Artists choosing to serve the local church are living with enormous pressure to use their talents and resources to achieve success, rather than simply creating art that connects with God's movement in their communities. In many cases, these expectations can cripple the local artists, forcing them to become an echo rather than a voice.

Creating makes me feel alive. I love writing songs and sharing them! I love playing piano and singing. My healing began with acknowledging what I love doing and releasing myself from the burden of comparing myself to others. When we clothe ourselves with the identity we have in Christ instead of with what others think of us (or what we *think* others think of us), we can have new freedom to be what God created us to be — and to create with abandon, as God intended.

Oh artist, you are loved by God. Step into your calling, but do not compare yourself to others. Do not let the number of downloads others have received, their bank balance, or whether they are recorded distract you from the worship and mission of God (Galatians 6:4–5). You are on your own path. Clothe yourself with your Christian identity: an artist created by God for his glory to create beauty that fulfills his mission in the world.

Meditate further: Genesis 3; Galatians 5

APPLICATION

Ask the Holy Spirit to reveal to you any place in your heart where you are comparing yourself to others. Our thoughts influence our actions. Do you need to confess and break the bondage of sin in any area? *Confess* your unholy thoughts. *Forgive* those who have influenced you into thought patterns. *Renounce* the devil's lies. He has no power over you! You have the authority in Christ to break the patterns and bondage you are in.

PRAYER

Adapted from Psalm 139

> Search me, O God, and know my heart
> Test me, and know my thoughts
> Reveal to me my evil ways
> And lead me into life.

Amen

Humility That Harms

BY HUNTER LYNCH

Do nothing from selfish ambition or conceit,
but in humility count others more significant than yourselves.

— PHILIPPIANS 2:3

As a musician and writer, I am well acquainted with the conflict between wanting to appear humble and wanting to appear productive. This inner battle, for the longest time, resulted in plentiful output in songwriting but stagnant exposure in song performing. I felt gifted to write but was too selfish to show anyone what I was working on. I was searching for this unachievable level of self-detachment, where this precious thing I was inspired to create would somehow be returned back to God without a smudge of selfish pride still attached. On paper? Honorable. In practice? Sinful.

Let me clarify what I'm getting at here. By no means am I advocating for an egotistical approach to creative practice. Humility still has a vital place at the heart of all we do, and we must realize that any iota of creative desire that overtakes us, to make something new that wasn't there before, is wholly due to God's kindness and ingenuity. We need humility to collaborate, to construct, and even to tear down to make room for something better. However, there is such a thing as *sinful* humility, and it is just as dangerous as blatant pride. Where pride would take something God-given and use it for personal glory, sinful humility takes what God gives and, through passive inactivity, simply throws it away. Make no mistake, if you wait for your heart to be "right" before you introduce that song to your local congregation, or read your poetry in front of a crowd, that moment will never come, and the gift will be wasted.

"Leaf by Niggle" is a tale from the pen of J. R. R. Tolkien that encapsulates the spirit of creative procrastination mixed with over-scrutiny of one's own work. It's a wonderful short story for any artist in need of comfort and inspiration. The main character, Niggle, spends his entire existence striving after an unachievable artistic goal (in this case, a grandiose painting). The busyness of daily life and his own slothful tendencies leave him with unfinished projects and unfulfilled longing. Though the ending is not unhappy, the story ends with Niggle's home and belongings being picked over after his death. This ending scene bears a line of dialogue that haunts me: " 'Oh, poor little Niggle!' said Perkins. 'Never knew he painted!' "

With this story in mind, I wonder how many of us will go about our lives as artists unknown by the world. What glory is yet to be yielded to the Lord? What song, painting, or poem has yet to be revealed to a world desperate for beauty? What I had to realize about my inner struggle between humility and transparency was that I would never fulfill my calling if I waited for my flesh to catch up with my desire to serve. I'm reminded of the parable of the talents in Matthew 25 and the harsh rebuke directed at the servant who buried what he had. That is a fate worth fleeing and a call to everyone God equips to steward those gifts well.

So herein lies the invitation: that together, we would strive toward work that renders glory solely unto the Lord, as broken and as pride-tinged as those efforts may be. There is nothing more dangerous to the Enemy than Spirit-empowered creativity unfettered by fear.

Meditate further: Psalm 144; Mark 12:41–44

APPLICATION

Ask God to bring to your mind some work or project of yours that you have kept to yourself. Ask him to show you your motives for keeping your work in the dark. Is it unfinished? Is it unrefined? Or are you simply worried about how it will be received?

Ask the Holy Spirit to grant you the wisdom and introspection needed to know the difference between creative apprehension and the creative process. Ask the Lord to remind you of hidden gems that have gathered dust over the years that are begging to be polished and shared. Ask for the courage to push those finished efforts into the light, that you may be obedient to his calling and diligent with his gift to you.

PRAYER

> I love you, O Lord my strength, my God who trains my hands for the tasks set before me. You are my rock and my fortress. Kindle in me a desire to know you. Reveal to me where fear is hindering my obedience to you. Grant me courage to share the gifts you have given me in true humility, and till the soil of my heart to receive your joy.
>
> *Amen*

Success and the Local Songwriter

BY CATHERINE MILLER & MOSES KIMANI

"And you shall love the Lord your God with all your heart and with all your soul and with all your mind and with all your strength."

— MARK 12:30

For a long time, I (Catherine) saw success as the perfect performance. A performance was to be without flaws, and success was measured by my worldly standards of attendance figures, budgets, number of albums, and the monetary equivalent. Jesus calls us to a different standard of success. We are to love the Lord our God with all our heart, soul, mind, and strength (Luke 10:27), growing in love and obedience with his purposes for our lives.

The words below from Moses Kimani of Nairobi, Kenya, have meant a lot to me. They serve to help me orient my heart and vocation under God's view of success. In 2 Timothy 2:4, Paul reminds us to not get "entangled in civilian pursuits," since our aim is to please God, who enlisted us in his service. Remember this when the world tells you that you need to appeal to certain powers and subscribe to certain views of success. Bring your vocation under God's authority, and let the Holy Spirit lead you to do what he will with your work for his purposes for the building up of the Church. May our art serve to connect us to God the Creator and further his mission to make "all things new."

A WORD TO ARTISTS | MOSES KIMANI

First, *love God with all your heart and serve him with all your art.* Bring it all to him. While he is a perfect God, he is not a perfectionist. As you keep practicing your skill, you will notice that what you offer will improve with time and you will be happier with what you offer him. But bring before him what you have and the Lord will receive it. Here is a theological truth you can bank on: Every time you make art, you mirror the creativity of our Creator God. And every time you present your work of art to him as worship, he receives highest honor and glory.

Second, *write congregational songs.* There are many beautiful songs out there, but most of them are written with the super-gifted voice in mind. When such songs are sung in a congregational setting, they are mostly only sung as specials by specially gifted members of the congregation or by visiting artists. We need more songs that are specifically written with a singing congregation in mind. We need to stop entertaining our congregations and to start helping them find their voice, so that we all may raise a united voice of worship and adoration to the Lord our God.

Third, *write songs that address the theological issues of the present day.* I find that most of the songs that we sing do not address the theological issues of our day. For instance, we need songs that express the reality of the gifts of the Holy Spirit and how such gifts would operate in the life of the church. We need songs that address matters of race, class and social justice. We need songs that call us to missions in the context of a "global village" in which there still exist some unreached and unengaged peoples, a "global village" in which the sending nations are now in need of missionaries from the very nations to which they previously sent missionaries.

Fourth, don't only write celebratory, feel-good songs; *write songs that mirror the entire human experience.* Previously, church growth theorists taught that churches would grow if only celebratory songs of worship were sung. Now, close to three decades later, we know differently. We know that God is best glorified when we present before him everything that we are going through — our joys and sorrows alike. To present only one aspect of the human experience while ignoring the other is to dehumanize the worshipers. Consider this, that more than half of the entire content of the Psalms are songs of lament. We need songs of joy, songs of celebration, songs of adoration, songs of lament and songs of protest for social justice. This will inject much needed authenticity in congregational worship.

Finally, not every song has to be "commercially viable." *Don't write songs with commercial viability as your focus; write songs with vertical worship and congregational viability as your first goal.* Some of the songs you write will be sung only once, maybe even by only you. Some of the songs will be sung only by your local congregation. And if the Lord leads you down the path of recording and production, some of your songs might receive radio airplay and be purchased. Remember, make your music for the audience of one — the Creator God whose creativity you get to mirror as you make your own works of art.

Meditate further: Psalm 96; Colossians 3:1–17

APPLICATION

Communication with God is a two-way conversation. One way to listen to God is through journaling. Spend time in quiet, talking to God, and write down what you feel he's saying to you. It's not gospel, and it's not supposed to be, but it's a discipline that can help us quiet our minds and listen to what God might be saying to us. The advice provided above was addressed to songwriters, but it can be applied to other artistic expressions just as well. Here are some questions to help with reflection:

- What is your motivation for creating works of art?
- What are some ways you can create that would encourage the participation of others?
- What are some ways that you can create in order to enable others to "find their voice," to express themselves in worship?

Journal about these thoughts and find ways to practice them the next time you create.

PRAYER

Come, Holy Spirit. You see the depths of my heart; you know my inmost being. Reveal to me the crevices of my heart you wish to fill with your presence. Orient my mind and heart to your direction, so that I and the works of my hands may serve you and build up those around me, for your love's sake.

Amen

The Golden Calf

BY CATHERINE MILLER

"But my people did not listen to my voice;
Israel would not submit to me.
So I gave them over to their stubborn hearts…"

— PSALM 81:11, 12A

When does the work of our hands glorify God, and at what point does it become idolatry?

Beauty and craftsmanship matter to God, but are the offerings of our time and talents always honoring to him? The tabernacle and the golden calf were both beautiful and skillfully crafted, but why did one honor God while the other was found to be an abomination that needed to be destroyed?

The answer to these questions centers on the heart of worship and obedience. Our acts of creativity must fall in submission to Christ. The golden calf incident was idolatrous in nature because the Israelites began to worship the creation instead of the Creator, an act of disobedience (Exodus 20:3).

In my own life, I found that I was consistently making decisions to sacrifice my relationship with God as I pursued developing my craft.

This is a common theme among vocational artists: we are pushed to work so hard at our craft that arrogance, pride, and idolatry creep in, slowly taking over the place in our hearts that is reserved for Jesus.

The golden calf did not reflect the glory of God, though it was beautifully crafted and made with gold. The Israelites bowed, sang, and danced before the calf, and in so doing they broke the first commandment: "You shall have no other gods before me" (Exodus 20:3). Craftsmanship and skill are important to God (Exodus 31:1-11; Exodus 36; 1 Chronicles 15:22, 25:7–8), but so are our hearts and our intention in creation. The Israelites turned to the golden calf because they doubted God's faithfulness, and so they took matters into their own hands.

Anything has the potential to become an idol and replace God in our worship, both personal and corporate. God does not depend on our creations to do his work. Rather, he invites us to use our abilities to carry out his mission of healing in the world. Our creativity must be centered on obedience to God's call on our lives. Our artistic creativity begins with our relationship with God, and our artistic decisions must be fueled by that union. Let your relationship with God inspire your creations. Pray before you create: Ask the Holy Spirit for guidance and for opportunities to share your stories and your work. Give your work to him and submit your creativity to his leadership, his timing, and his uses.

An artistic life rooted in the worship of God begins with the disciplines of prayer, Scripture reading, and connection to a corporate body for worship. Through these disciplines, we can discern the direction God may want us to take as artists. Let your personal worship of God fuel your creation of art for public worship. Let us recommit our vocations and creations to him who saved and redeemed us with his broken body and shed blood. Let us study the Word, alone and with others, because what we believe shapes our songs, our stories, and ourselves.

Meditate further: Exodus 20; Hebrews 8

APPLICATION

Meditate on Psalm 139:1–4. Ponder your recent thoughts, actions, and words. What motivations, desires, or fears do they demonstrate?

Read Psalm 139:23–24 as a personal prayer to God. Invite God the Holy Spirit to examine your heart. As God shows you areas of your life in which you are putting other things before him, ask the Spirit to help you submit those areas to God and rest in his power and provision.

PRAYER

Lord, lead me in the path of righteousness. May what I create serve to glorify you. May I, your sheep, hear your voice and respond when you call. I was created to glorify you, God. May I grow in my union with you, for you are the Lord God who created me and gave me life. Fill me with your vision to do your work in the world.

Amen

Confidence in Christ

BY RACHEL WILHELM

And we all, with unveiled face, beholding the glory of the Lord, are
being transformed into the same image from one degree of glory to another.
For this comes from the Lord who is the Spirit.

— 2 CORINTHIANS 3:18

It took me a long time to say out loud, "I am a musician." It took me even longer to say, "I am an artist." I always knew I could say these things about myself, but I was afraid of what others would think of me if I admitted it, and even more afraid of what they would expect of me if I did. What if I start to sing and they hate my singing voice? What if they notice that I don't practice my scales? What if they think my lyrics stink? What if they think, "Who does she think she is, anyway?!" With all the little jabs and stabs of criticism I received over the years, these "what ifs" just grew bigger and bigger until I felt paralyzed by my own imaginings. And they were exactly that — imaginings. Let me explain.

Such is the confidence that we have through Christ toward God. Not that we are sufficient in ourselves to claim anything as coming from us, but our sufficiency is from God, who has made us sufficient to be ministers of a new covenant, not of the letter but of the Spirit. For the letter kills, but the Spirit gives life.... But when one turns to the Lord, the veil is removed. Now the Lord is the Spirit, and where the Spirit of the Lord is, there is freedom. And we all, with unveiled face, beholding the glory of the Lord, are being transformed into the same image from one degree of glory to another. For this comes from the Lord who is the Spirit.

— 2 Corinthians 3:4–6, 16–18

We are made in the image of God, and we are being transformed. We are not sufficient in ourselves, and we cannot claim anything good as originating from ourselves. God is doing the good work, transforming, working, creating. God made me a musician and an artist. End of story. This is sufficient for God, so why not for me? If anyone has a problem with that, they need to take it up with him!

My two favorite saints who learned confidence are Gideon and Moses. Gideon questions God when the angel of the Lord declares that he is with him and calls Gideon a mighty man of valor. Gideon argues that he is just a lowly member of his family from a small tribe and that he has not done anything valiant. But look at what God does through him! He uses Gideon to miraculously deliver the Israelites from the oppressive Midianites.

Moses is very similar. When told by the Lord, speaking from a burning bush, to go to Egypt to deliver the Israelites, Moses argues with God, asserting that he lacks the qualities of the leader God is looking for: he is not articulate, no one will believe him, and oh, Lord, please send someone else. But God knew what Moses could become if he learned to rely solely on the power of God.

I spent years wrestling with my own insecurities. I wore myself out with prayer and supplication, trying to understand God's love and his delight in me as his child. It is his lovingkindness and steadfast love that eventually became my firm foundation. Now I can truly believe what Scripture says about who I am in Jesus, and I can recognize the trap of insecurity.

Be confident in the calling God has for you. He has fashioned you with your own unique creative leanings and desires for you to use for his glory — not of your own sufficiency, but of his. His desire is to see you flourish in the wellspring of his likeness, stepping into his will for your life confident, satisfied, and unafraid. "For we are his workmanship, created in Christ Jesus for good works, which God prepared beforehand, that we should walk in them" (Ephesians 2:10).

Meditate further: Jeremiah 1; Ephesians 2:1–10

APPLICATION

Write down a list of all your insecurities, even the ones that make you very uncomfortable and embarrassed. Confess them to the Lord. Then look at each insecurity and write down what God says about you instead of what you say about yourself. Pray that the mind of Christ will dwell in you richly and keep you safe in the security and confidence he promises.

PRAYER

Lord, I lift all of my insecurities to you. I know that where I am weak, you are strong. Give me the courage to walk in your will. Help me to have confidence in who you made me to be and the work you have given me to do. Give me that contentment that is only reached by having satisfaction in you. In Jesus' name,

Amen

Craftmanship

BY HUNTER LYNCH

Sing to him a new song; play skillfully on the strings, with loud shouts.

— PSALM 33:3

When considering the world of guitars, why would one instrument cost $100 and another cost over $2,000? For those outside of the vicious need/want cycle of musical instruments, it may be difficult to explain. However, the pennies and dimes eventually come down to one thing: the presence or absence of craftsmanship. On the one hand, you have what is basically a mass-produced toy sold at the local Walmart, and on the other, you have an instrument that bears the sweat and blood of a woodworker — a brave soul who may or may not have allowed a few choice words to fill the hollow body of the acoustic guitar you'll be leading worship with next Sunday. A human being made in the image of God poured himself (or herself) into this creation, and the price tag normally reflects that truth. This is why we invest substantially into things we consider important: We know that what is done well will last — that it has intrinsic value.

In Exodus 35, we see this principle play out in the construction of the tabernacle. Not everyone is asked to contribute; in fact, only those whose particular skill set aligned with the need were asked to join in.

The tabernacle was to be crafted well; excellence was the standard in this creation process.

Last, consider Psalm 8, in which God is vividly described as a masterful Creator. David writes that when he observes the majesty of God's handiwork, his thoughts instantly turn to humility and reverence, as he asks, "What is man that you are mindful of him, and the son of man that you care for him?" The glory of the Lord fills the Earth, and it is not unreasonable to believe that God is calling us to emulate him as we labor for excellence.

As we turn our attention to our individual creative processes, the question must be asked, "How much am I sweating over this? How am I laboring to ensure that this song/poem/painting isn't just a carbon copy of my immediate influences but is a vivid representation of a unique, God-given gifting?" We have been given our marching orders — to build and contribute to the church — yet we must decide to what degree we will be committed. Will we produce our work thoughtlessly, as a mechanized factory does, or will we allow the sweat stains to be visible in the grain?

May we strive, through our best and worst efforts, to cast aside the shortcuts and embrace the slowness of hammer striking chisel, unveiling beauty with unyielding persistence.

Meditate further: Exodus 35:4–29; Ephesians 1

APPLICATION

Examine your most recent works (a song, poem, or painting) and ask yourself the following questions:

- How well have I labored over this work? Can I "see the sweat"?
- How can I refine it? Where are my weak spots?
- Have I shown this to others, to receive a broad spectrum of feedback? How am I implementing their advice?

These are practical steps to rightly discern whether or not your finished product is actually finished! Never hang up the pen, and always be open to letting the work of art become what it needs to become.

PRAYER

> Father, I praise you for your majestic works — not simply for creating, but for doing so beautifully. For where there could be barren plains, you graced us with fields of color. Where a placid pond at stream's end would do just as well, you gave the wonder of the waterfall. O God who gives more and better, instruct me today to see canyons in my plateau, to see mountains instead of uniformity, and to see redemption's story unfolding in my meager efforts. Strengthen me now to set my hands to a labor that will reach beyond this life and, by your grace, may nourish generations to come.
>
> *Amen*

Cultivating Gifts Through Trial

BY NATHANAEL ORR

Count it all joy, my brothers, when you meet trials
of various kinds, for you know that the testing of
your faith produces steadfastness.

— JAMES 1:2–3

So often, when trials come, we experience a scarcity mindset. We imagine that our existence is somewhat lacking. Our present woes and pains make us view the world in dim tones of gray, leading us to think, "If only something changed, then the color would return."

Have you experienced those minor-key moments? Perhaps you're in one now. But consider James 1:2–4: "Count it all joy, my brothers, when you meet trials of various kinds, for you know that the testing of your faith produces steadfastness. And let steadfastness have its full effect, that you may be perfect and complete, lacking in nothing." Suppose trials are not meant to dim the light that brings your life color but are actually rare and powerful opportunities to bring true color to your world! Nothing speaks of a life full of rich vibrancy more than the words "pure joy." And yet notice how, in this passage, pure joy is linked to "trials of many kinds"? Isn't that wondrous and strange!

As I write, I have my five-day-old baby girl sleeping next to me in her Moses basket, a perfect example of the fruit that comes through suffering — the pains of labor. I can testify that even the simple act of waiting can be almost unbearable, a trial in and of itself, as baby Emily was eleven days overdue, making every day feel like a year. But if you could see how Emily's siblings smile as they stroke her soft cheeks, you would feel as I do, that the fruit was worth the wait.

Another type of suffering occurs in wartime. During a world war, there are frontlines drawn all over the countries of the globe, and the closer you are to one of those, the more your senses pick up the signs of battle. You can see flashes in the dark skies, hear gunshots and explosions, smell the burning buildings, feel the earth quaking. Likewise, the further away you are, the less you can sense the battles raging in the world.

The passage in James encourages us to sense the battle. Why? Because in God's economy, that is where true fruitfulness is! That is where God truly cultivates his precious gifts in you — "that you may be perfect and complete, lacking in nothing." Therefore, consider it pure joy to sense your trials, for God turns graves into gardens and battle-fields into places of his victory!

So, to encourage you, I invite you to imagine that God turns the tables on your suffering, and instead of taking you away from the battleground, leads you to it — to a place where enemies are vanquished and your gifts are cultivated amid tests, trials, and suffering.

A final challenge: If your senses can't grasp the battle — if you feel like someone in a country village hundreds of miles away from the frontlines in the city — then the false vibrancy of human comfort and security might be more dulling than you realize.

Meditate further: Psalm 86; Hebrews 12

APPLICATION

Consider expressing key points of trial or pain in your life through your preferred art medium. You could pen a song about your battle with sin or paint on canvas your traumatic experience. As you do, consider prayerfully exploring how God's victory over that situation is interwoven with the hardships you face. Discuss with God how the difficulties now are a part of his plan to give you pure joy and cultivate his gift of increased faith in your life. Let the Spirit preach to your soul of God's salvation amid your trials.

PRAYER

Read or sing this psalm as a prayer.

> Be merciful to me, my God,
>> for my enemies are in hot pursuit;
>> all day long they press their attack.
> My adversaries pursue me all day long;
>> in their pride many are attacking me.
> When I am afraid, I put my trust in you.
> In God, whose word I praise —
> in God I trust and am not afraid.
>> What can mere mortals do to me?
>>> — Psalm 56:1–4

Amen

When No Ideas Come

BY STEPHEN SLOSS

> *But, as it is written, "What no eye has seen, nor ear heard,*
> *nor the heart of man imagined, what God has prepared for those*
> *who love him" — these things God has revealed to us through the Spirit.*
> *For the Spirit searches everything, even the depths of God.*

— 1 CORINTHIANS 2:9-10

All too often, I find myself staring at the screen or a piece of blank paper waiting for inspiration — praying for a word, a sign, a hook, or an image. Another hour goes by as I noodle on my guitar. No tune emerges. Sound familiar?

When this happens, I take comfort in the passage from 1 Corinthians. We have the Holy Spirit of God with us. *Always* with us. Our thoughts may be understood by our own spirit, but the Holy Spirit within us understands God's thoughts, so our thoughts can be prompted and influenced directly by the Holy Spirit. This is why Paul says we have the mind of Christ.

In Romans 12:2, Paul coaches us to be transformed by the renewing of our minds as a precondition to being in the best place to hear God's voice in our thoughts. We have everything we need to be inspired, influenced, and directed by God each day. So why do we struggle to put it into practice?

Many of us struggle to believe that God communicates with us in our thoughts. We might also be so distracted by our busy lives — and our worries, obsessions, and passions — that we don't give the Spirit enough room in our thoughts. No wonder God often calls us to be still, and to stop and listen.

On the other hand, the expectations we place on ourselves can be too high. We strive too hard. We criticize ourselves and our creativity. We compare ourselves to others when we should not.

In the Old Testament, the nation of Israel was well known at times for the wrong reasons: disobedience, stiff necks, and hard-heartedness. Are we guilty of anything similar? Is there anything standing between us and God today? Seek forgiveness. We will struggle to hear God's thoughts and inspiration without first confessing our sins and receiving his forgiveness.

Meditate further: Psalm 63; Romans 8

APPLICATION

Take the next ten minutes to be still. Close your eyes, breathe slowly, and rest in the presence of God. Read Psalm 139:14:

> I praise you, for I am fearfully and wonderfully made.
> Wonderful are your works;
> > my soul knows it very well.

PRAYER

Father God, I thank you that I am fearfully and wonderfully made. Holy Spirit, inspire my creativity today. Talk with me in my thoughts. Jesus, be at the center of all I do and say today and always.

Amen

Light in the Darkness

BY CATHERINE MILLER

> *"Therefore I will not restrain my mouth;*
> *I will speak in the anguish of my spirit;*
> *I will complain in the bitterness of my soul."*

— JOB 7:11

What do we do when the world feels uncertain and our path seems unclear?

The Bible offers us a model in the Psalms of how to carry our pain, worry, distress, uncertainty, fears, and anxieties to God.

Lament is crying out to God in our sadness, anger, and pain and asking God to fix it. Most of the psalms of lament turn to hope, but Psalm 88 sits in grief, and it isn't until Psalm 89 that the psalmist's perspective changes. Verses 13 through 18 of Psalm 88 read,

> But I, O LORD, cry to you;
>   in the morning my prayer comes before you.
> O LORD, why do you cast my soul away?
>   Why do you hide your face from me?
> Afflicted and close to death from my youth up,

I suffer your terrors; I am helpless.
Your wrath has swept over me;
  your dreadful assaults destroy me.
They surround me like a flood all day long;
  they close in on me together.
You have caused my beloved and my friend to shun me;
  my companions have become darkness.

The Psalms show us how to bring our emotions into worship. Song-writer Wendell Kimbrough says that "what we don't bring into worship doesn't get formed by Jesus. I want to be able to bring my immature anger to church and have it formed and shaped by liturgy.... I'm feeling all this stuff, but I don't know what to do with it. I needed the container of the psalms, the language, to form this anger into something that wasn't sinful, rebellious, or distant from God."

As artists, part of living out our calling is creating, even when we're sad, angry, anxious, and fearful. King David, the attributed author of many of the Psalms, was an artist, after all — a poet and a musician.

I encourage you to see your creativity as *light*. Light in a world of darkness. Light inspired by God's truth, goodness, and beauty. As our hearts are formed in worship, we become more like Jesus. We become the light to the world. Part of our calling as artists is to use our creativity to share that light with our churches and communities, be it in person and local, or online with your friends on social media.

So what do we do when the world feels uncertain and our path seems unclear?

We worship God, privately and corporately, reading Scripture and liturgy, singing and songwriting, painting and dancing, baking and gardening, in response to the Word. This is our spiritual warfare: creativity, inspired by our union with God. We bring all our worries to the God who created us, bringing them to him in worship and letting him form our hearts. Then the Spirit can inspire our creativity and release it back into the world so that we might inspire others.

In the words of Andrew Peterson,

> This is why the Enemy wants you to think you have no song to write, no story to tell, no painting to paint. He wants to quiet you. So sing. Let the Word by which the Creator made you fill your imagination, guide your pen, lead you from note to note until a melody is strung together like a glimmering constellation in the clear sky (*Adorning the Dark*, 183).

Meditate further: Psalm 116; John 8:12–30

APPLICATION

The following is a blessing from the Kenyan Rite, an Anglican liturgical service. The physical action of sweeping the arm helps to embody the sending of our problems and difficulties to Christ and is a key part of preparing for the mission of God. We need Christ to take upon himself all the problems of our lives so that he can handle them, and we do this in corporate worship so that he can form our hearts for God's mission (Philippians 4:6–7; Isaiah 41:10).

All our problems
We send to the cross of Christ.
All our difficulties
We send to the cross of Christ.
All the devil's works
We send to the cross of Christ.
All our hopes
We set on the risen Christ.

PRAYER

Light of the world, your light shines greater than the sun. Keep our eyes fixed on you, so that our creativity may be a light to our communities. Use our work to bless those around us and bring honor to you, O God, through the work of the Son and the Holy Spirit.

Amen

Worship as Warfare

BY MELISSA AMBER MCKINNEY

And when they began to sing and praise, the LORD set
an ambush against [the great multitude of their attackers].

— 2 CHRONICLES 20:22

In 2 Chronicles 20, God's people are under attack. A "great multitude" is on its way with plans to destroy them. They are outnumbered and afraid: they are in the land that God had promised, and simultaneously, at risk (or so it seemed), of losing that very land.

Maybe you find yourself in a similar place, having experienced the promises of God but facing your personal enemies and demons, crying out for God to "deliver [you] from evil" but feeling that God is bailing on answering the very prayer Jesus taught us to pray. Or perhaps you question whether you have ever tangibly experienced God's promises at all, because you haven't ever had a palpable sense of God's deliverance or favor or presence.

We've all been there at some point. Overwhelmed, exhausted, and afraid, echoing the psalmist as we cry, "How long, oh Lord?" Like Jehoshaphat, we may be asking, "Are you not God in heaven?" When we're fired because of a malicious coworker or when another unarmed

Black person or an unborn baby is killed, perhaps our prayer resonates even more closely with him: "O our God, will you not execute judgment on them?" Maybe you live in a country where people are being martyred, and you must keep your faith a secret from the government. I would venture to say that most of us reading this are not under attack in the traditional sense, but even if we are unaware, we, like ancient Israel, are at war: "For we do not wrestle against flesh and blood, but against the rulers, against the authorities, against the cosmic powers over this present darkness, against the spiritual forces of evil in the heavenly places" (Ephesians 6:12). As members of the kingdom of God, we are on the front lines of a spiritual battle.

In light of that attack, I believe Jehoshaphat has much to teach us. When I am afraid and tempted to doubt the goodness of God, I may unintentionally give the enemy a foothold. In fact, even when I clearly see the enemy on the horizon and I'm noticeably outnumbered and outgunned, my first inclination is to pull away from God. I may doubt his faithfulness, fight by myself, look to other saviors, or binge Netflix, all to avoid my struggles with sin or dull the ache in my heart that injustice continues in the world.

Jehoshaphat, on the other hand, took a step closer. He didn't try to figure it out on his own or create an ungodly alliance, as other people of God had done so many times before. Instead, he went to God and reiterated all of God's promises to him, and then he did a counterintuitive thing: he worshipped. God declared through a prophet that Judah did not need to fear, that God himself would fight for them, and that in fact it was his battle. Jehoshaphat believed, and I'm sure that, like Abraham, his belief "was counted to him as righteousness," but then he did an even more counterintuitive and irrational thing: he commanded that his army be preceded on the battlefield by an unarmed, robed chorus: "And when [Jehoshaphat] had taken counsel with the people, he appointed those who were to sing to the LORD and praise him in holy attire, as they went before the army, and say, "Give thanks to the LORD, for his steadfast love endures forever" (2 Chronicles 20:21) — and God showed up! The Lord prevailed by sovereignly intervening and making Judah's enemies fight each other. He brought victory to his people as they obeyed his command to not fear, but to stand firm.

Ephesians 6 uses a similar command, telling those of us fighting our spiritual battles to put on our spiritual armor and to "stand firm." As a worship artist, I can't help but see my songwriting as a means of putting on the spiritual armor referenced in Ephesians 6. In our worship and our creation of worship art, we reflect upon and steep our minds in the gospel, putting on the helmet of salvation. We put things into perspective with the truth — the belt that holds our armor together. We articulate the faith, our shield against the flaming darts of the enemy of our souls. Our hearts are protected by our breastplate of righteousness imputed to us by Christ himself, who "knew no sin" but became sin "so that in him we might become the righteousness of God" (2 Corinthians 5:21). We proclaim *shalom*, and the very shoes upon our feet help to spread the peace that we've been given, and we wield the only offensive piece of the armor, our sword of the Spirit. That sword is the Word of God, which inspires us and becomes the reference point by which we gauge our art.

We put on the armor and stand firm, for the battle is the Lord's.

Meditate further: Psalm 48; Revelation 7

APPLICATION

Read the passages above and reflect on the following questions:

· Do I believe that God wants me to see victory in the current battles I am fighting?

· If not, what would it look like to believe that he does?

67

- God has placed us in spiritual family. Whom could I ask to join me in my battle?
- How have I seen God wage war for me in the past?
- What would it look like for me to put on my armor and stand firm?

Then go and create. Remember, believers prevail in the battle "by the blood of the Lamb and by the word of their testimony" (Revelation 12:11). Your testimony can include the expressed substance of your story in the written word or on a canvas or in a carefully crafted tune.

PRAYER

Dear Father, attune my spirit to the battle going on around me. Open my heart to know your love for me and your desire to protect me. Open my eyes to see how you are fighting for me. Empower me to put on my armor, and give me courage to stand firm. Help me to keep the faith even in war. Thank you for your faithfulness, for all that you've done, are doing, and are going to do.

Amen

Artistry and the Great Commission

BY HUNTER LYNCH

To the weak I became weak, that I might win the weak. I have become all things to all people, that by all means I might save some. I do it all for the sake of the gospel, that I may share with them in its blessings.

— 1 CORINTHIANS 9:22-23

In Paul's first letter to the church in Corinth, we see an outline for the early church, from directions on the structure of church leadership to how to handle food sacrificed to idols. But there's one section that particularly demands our attention because it is relevant to the work of the artist within the body of Christ. In 1 Corinthians 9:19–23, we see Paul's ministry being shaped by contextual awareness. For the sake of the gospel, Paul models an attitude about ministry that we can mimic today — that we should allow a level of mindful collaboration between the people we are ministering to and our own art, with which we minister to the body.

In order to accomplish this mission effectively, there must be two elements in our creation that work in tandem: approachability and beauty. When we create for the edification of the body of Christ, we are putting missional feet to our work. We're setting up an "on ramp" for unbelievers to take (we hope), and we're presenting a picture that the most seasoned Christians can revel in. This is a wholly different creative process than "writing to sell," especially when considering solo projects that tend to take more liberties with lyricism and musicianship. Even in the world of art, this principle applies. The people we minister to need tangible things that they can grasp and that can point them to Jesus, not works that come across as aloof and pretentious.

Yet beauty must remain in healthy tension with simplicity! We come into contact with believers and nonbelievers alike who are hungry for truth and beauty to grab their attention and turn their hearts upward. In an interview with prolific singer-songwriter Andrew Peterson on the Resound Worship Songwriting Podcast (episode 80), Joel Payne inquired about Peterson's songwriting process. Part of Andrew's response highlights the music scene in Nashville, where artists don't have to "like" the music they write, and most just throw things at the wall to see what sticks. I don't envy their task in the least! When we create out of compulsion, jotting down throwaway lines and throwing away our individuality, we end up with half-done art that, while its meaning is plain, doesn't give the listener or observer much reason to praise our Father in Heaven.

The challenge, then, is to engage our hearts and minds in the act of creation for the sake of the people we minister to. Every word, every brushstroke, must aim for a peculiar beauty that is tempered by the community in which we serve. This is a difficult process that demands our utmost effort, and we may be asked to cut the line we love the most for the sake of clarity, or to build our piece around an idea that is less nebulous and more down-to-earth. Yet we press on, and we do it all for the sake of the gospel, that Christ may be brought glory and that his Church may expand and be edified.

Meditate further: Genesis 1:28–31; Matthew 28:16–20

APPLICATION

Consider how you partner with your church in a creative capacity. Are you thinking about using your gift in a corporate setting? Challenge yourself to do the following:

1. Critically pore over the proposed work. Ask yourself, "Would the average person in my context understand this, or does it demand extensive explanation?"

2. Find people you trust, believers and nonbelievers, and ask for their honest opinion of what you're working on. Both perspectives are valuable and indispensable tools for the artist.

3. Pray! Pray that the Holy Spirit would guide your work, and that the object of your rigorous labor would bring souls to Christ and evoke praise from his saints.

PRAYER

O God, we bring our gifts to you today in humble submission. Open our eyes to the need around us, where lack and want would seek dominion. Holy Spirit, empower us to press against this emptiness with the weapons you have deemed fit to place in our hands, shaping every creative labor. May we fear not the critic's tongue, the pride that lingers within, or the looming cloud of rejection. Instead, embolden our hearts to fear your name, that we may form great creations to fulfill the Great Commission.

Amen

The Calling in the Crushing

BY MELISSA AMBER MCKINNEY

The Spirit of God has made me, and the breath of the Almighty gives me life.

— JOB 33:4

During my first breakup, I wrote my first song, "Breath of Life," a declaration of who God is:

> You are the air I'm breathing in.
> You are the water of my soul.
> I need You to survive.
> Knew me before the world began,
> created me as who I am,
> that's how I began
> with Your breath of life.

Although I wouldn't have identified it at thirteen, I was writing modern-day psalms. Years later, when my dad left our home without a word, my grief was palpable. On more than one occasion, I was so distraught that I paced and cried during the music at church. One time in particular, I caught the eye of a visiting pastor. Moved in his spirit, he spoke a word over my life: he saw me as a painting that God was carefully creating and intending to put on display. Later, in another time of great pain over my mental illness, I received another image — a crystal, shaped like me, with God's light shining through. I didn't recognize it then, but I see clearly now that God was revealing my calling. My life was meant to create beauty.

English composer Frederick Delius wrote, "Music is an outburst of the soul." It is obvious that music has been a means of powerful expression for my soul. But to what end? According to Thomas Aquinas, "A song is the exultation of the mind dwelling on eternal things, bursting forth in the voice." The hardship of our lives primes us for those outbursts of sorrow and joy, and songs and poems allow us to transcend our present sufferings by shifting our focus to the eternal. They give us the ability to fulfill our "chief end," to both glorify and enjoy God forever. They recenter our lives, reorder our hearts, and reset our minds on truth:

> You are my strength when I feel weak and weary.
> You are the sun when life gets dark and dreary,
> the only one who shows your love for me so clearly.

Like David, our songs are the product of conversations with our souls, reminders of the true Source of our hope. They are ebenezers of God's faithfulness and manifestations of our faith — "the assurance of things hoped for, the conviction of things not seen." I will never forget how God met me in that breakup, because the lyrics of that song bring me back to remembrance of his extravagant love for me:

> You know the number of the stars in the sky.
> You bottle up the tears that fall from my eyes.
> That I might live you gave your only Son to die.

In the last twenty years, since I wrote those lyrics, I've seen more highs and lows. Music has been a means of processing doubt, dealing with a mood disorder, and confronting God in times of lament. Many times I've been tempted to believe that the obstacles I go through hinder my calling, but God uses the despairing moments to give "beauty for ashes." It's been invaluable to have the skills to create while in the winepress, during the pressure-forming-diamond moments. These painful times have shaped my capacity for empathy and led me to my current work as a peer in mental health, but they haven't just refined my character and honed my relational ministry. They have shaped me into a worship artist.

I don't remember exactly why I started singing, but I know that I keep singing and writing partly because of my pain. In the words of John Piper, "The greatest songs are born of the greatest suffering."

In this time, it is paramount for worship artists like us to remember that our struggles do not disqualify us, but rather have the potential to bring us closer to God, refine us, and lead us to honest worship in hard times. The sufferings we go through can be strokes in the painting that God is putting on display, beauty he gives us for ashes, whispers of our calling.

Meditate further: Isaiah 61:1–7; Mark 14

APPLICATION

Reflect and "trace the rainbow through the rain" ("Oh Love that Will Not Let Me Go" by 19th-century hymnwriter George Matheson). How has God used your suffering for your good (Romans 8:28)? Dwell upon those moments and thank God for them.

Sometimes we aren't able to see God's purposes on this side of heaven. Ask God if you need to lament instead. If so, take time to express your honest frustration or sadness or hurt to the Lord. Lament is a legitimate form of worship.

PRAYER

Remember me, O Lord, in my distress. Even when I walk through "the valley of the shadow of death," I know you are near. Bring peace to my mind and comfort to my soul. Send me friends to point me to the truth of your Word and remind me of your goodness when I am depressed and depleted.

Amen

Kintsugi People in a Fractured World

BY ELISE MASSA

The Lord builds up Jerusalem; he gathers the outcasts of Israel.
He heals the brokenhearted and binds up their wounds.

— PSALM 147:2-3

For the last several months, I have been listening to the Culture Care podcast, "Light Through the Cracks," hosted by Brianna Kinsman and Makoto Fujimura. The pilot episode unpacks the concepts of culture care, art, faith, and the art of *kintsugi*. Kintsugi is a traditional Japanese art form in which kintsugi masters mend broken pottery using lacquer and gold. Kinsman describes the process of kintsugi as follows: First, name the fracture; second, see the landscapes that arise from the fractures; third, sand down the edges; and fourth, join the pieces together with gold and lacquer.

I believe that the kintsugi art form has significant applications to those called to a vocation in music and worship arts, and to the church as a whole. We have the opportunity to live in a broken world as *kintsugi people*. Artist Makoto Fujimura shares this reflection on his website:

You see, when you create and make into the fissures of life — when you rebuild from a devastating fire — when you create, despite scarcity — when you "consider the lilies" (Matthew 6), especially when you are afraid — then God chooses those moments to reveal God's Presence in our lives. We are makers, as our God is our Maker. God did not promise us an easy life but promised us an abundant one — an abundant life of creativity and imaginative freedom.

Fujimura goes on to speak these prophetic words to us:

> Your generation will mend and pour gold into the fissures of our broken times. And you can not only mend; you can create anew, create a world in which an invitation will be given to those who are broken. Those who mourn, those who are persecuted and those who are poor in spirit will be offered a great light. Your lives can be an offering of peace in a divided time — a gesture of hope for those in despair. Your sacrifice will be an aroma of the New. So go mend. Be the kintsugi masters of your generation, of your own disciplines, in your workplaces, and in your homes. Pour gold into the fissures of the world.

This is my prayer for you: Become a kintsugi master in the world around you. Name the fractures. Imagine the redemptive landscapes that can arise as you radiate Christ's light and glory. Work out your faith and art with fear and trembling as the Spirit sands and sanctifies the rough edges. And then, go mend.

But do not go alone. Join with the creative community of artistic disciples — poets, visual artists, songwriters, novelists, dancers, designers — who use their craft to point to the true Creator of us all. We would love to share this sacred space with you.

Meditate further: Isaiah 61:8–11; Revelation 22

APPLICATION

Mosaics are another form of art that speaks to the renewal of brokenness. There are many beautiful mosaics throughout the world. For this exercise, search for a picture of La Maison Picassiette in Chartres, France. The story of this house is intriguing: between 1938 and 1964, a graveyard sweeper gathered crude fragments as he walked the city. He took the pieces and assembled them into the house and grounds of La Maison Picassiette.

After you've found a picture of this house that is particularly striking to you, use these next steps of *visio divina* ("holy seeing") to ask the Holy Spirit to reveal his truths through this work of art.

1. Read Isaiah 61:1–4. Meditate on this scripture as you look at a mosaic. What area or element of the picture draws your attention?

2. Focus on that element. Ask the Lord why he is drawing your attention there. Listen in silence for one to five minutes.

3. Next, ask the Lord to speak to you. Does he have anything to tell you about this element? Listen in silence for one to five minutes.

4. Next, ask the Lord what he may be calling you to do with his revelation. Listen in silence for one to five minutes.

5. Finally, say a prayer of gratitude, using the one below or another from your heart.

PRAYER

Based on the collect A Renewer of Society, from The Book of Common Prayer *(2019)*

Almighty and everlasting God, you kindled the flame of your love in our hearts to show your compassion and mercy to the poor and the persecuted. Grant your humble servants an increase of faith and power, with love, righteous zeal, and gratitude for the example of such renewal work from those saints who came before us; through Jesus Christ our Lord, who lives and reigns with you and the Holy Spirit, one God, forever and ever.

Amen

Stones of Fire

BY CATHERINE MILLER

As you come to him, a living stone rejected by men but in the sight of God chosen and precious, you yourselves like living stones are being built up as a spiritual house, to be a holy priesthood, to offer spiritual sacrifices acceptable to God through Jesus Christ.

— 1 PETER 2:4–5

Dear artists,

You are *stones of fire*. Filled with the Holy Spirit, you are precious, beautiful, unique gemstones in the eyes of the Lord. You were created for a purpose: not to mimic each other or the world, but to reflect the beautiful diversity and glory of God's creation in the universe. This means that the musical worship of churches in Tallahassee, Florida, might sound different from the worship in Beijing, China. The liturgy of Nairobi, Kenya, might be different from the liturgy in Thomasville, Georgia. *And that is okay. That is good. That is beautiful.*

United Adoration's leadership team is a diverse group of people representing multiple denominations. We serve in large churches and house churches, in church plants and cathedrals, in big cities and small towns. We are united by our love of creativity, healing, and craftsmanship. We are united by our love for the Triune God:

81

We believe in God the Father,

who is the Good Shepherd, who loves us, and who created a
    wonderful, diverse universe and saw that it was good.

We believe in Jesus Christ,

the only begotten Son of God, who fulfilled the law of God, died
    for our sins, rose from the grave, and ascended to his Father
    in heaven.

We believe in God the Holy Spirit,

who speaks to us and inspires our artistic work, and
    who brings healing to our souls.

As a movement, United Adoration works with artists and pastors to revitalize the creativity of the local church in order to minister to the Lord and his people. Through this work, artists are receiving healing, relationships are being strengthened between pastors and artists, leaders being raised up, and collaboration is taking place across cultures, denominations, and stylistic preferences.

A VISION OF UNITY

Our logo is a symbol of unity, inspired by the high priest's breastpiece described in Exodus 28. Adorning the breastpiece were twelve unique stones, arranged in four rows of three, representing the tribes of Israel. Engraved with seals on the stones were the names of each of the twelve tribes, and the high priest was given a curious instruction: he is to carry the names of all of Israel over his heart as a reminder before the Lord. The reminder, according to Baruch J. Schwartz, is a representation: The high priest comes before God representing all of Israel. Schwartz says, "...by wearing them when he entered the divine abode, the high priest embodied the entire community on whose behalf he came and called God's attention to their needs" ("Priestly Vestments" in *The Oxford Dic-*

tionary of the Jewish Religion, 546). As a movement, we feel a special calling to love artists and call attention to their needs.

These gemstones also symbolize the beauty and glory of God. James B. Jordan describes the gemstones as "stones of fire." White light refracts into brilliant colors in some gemstones, notably diamonds. The "fire" within, says Jordan, reflects the glory of God. "The High Priest, whose chest was covered with such fiery stones, thus had his own personal glory-cloud, an image of God's" (*Through New Eyes*, 75). We represent those gemstones today, dear Christians. As the living stones that make up the Church (1 Peter 2:5), we house the fire within: the Holy Spirit (Romans 8:9). It is under this banner that we can be united in adoration of the risen Christ, collaborating and creating alongside God and each other.

The symbolism of the gemstones draws us back to God's glory. As we are each unique people made in the image of God, our worship should reflect that uniqueness and beauty. We must resist the external pressure to homogenize our worship across cultures. Each of us has a unique calling and purpose in the kingdom of God; each of us reflects the glory and beauty of God in a way that may build up and bless the local church.

As United Adoration, we delight in working with local congregations, dioceses, regions, and movements to help release their unique cultural expressions of worship. Each body of believers has its own language, style, and artistic discipline, but we are united worldwide as part of the "one holy catholic and apostolic church" (the Nicene Creed).

A VISION OF COLLABORATION

The artist Bezalel was a man filled with the Holy Spirit. He also had the skills, ability, and knowledge in all kinds of crafts to accomplish his mission: fashioning the ark of the covenant, the tabernacle and all its furnishings, the anointing oils and fragrances used in worship, and the garments for the priests. He shaped artistic designs in gold, silver, and bronze; he cut and set stones; he carved wood.

The designs implemented for the construction of the tabernacle came from God himself. Carmen Joy Imes remarks, "God invites us to exercise creativity in many areas, but when it comes to his dwelling place, he's the designer-in-chief. Moses' job is simply to communicate the vision and ensure that it is carried out" (*Bearing God's Name,* 71). God designed his own spiritual house in the desert so he could dwell with his people; but his people, filled with the Holy Spirit, carried out those designs. The tabernacle was an exercise in artistic obedience.

Scripture also notes that Bezalel did not work alone: He and Oholiab worked together to teach other artisans. Then there is a beautiful vision as the Israelites came forward and offered their work to God: Skilled workers who knew how to carry out the work of the sanctuary came forward, a freewill offering of their skills to build this house of worship. The tabernacle was a collaborative artistic work of craftsmanship. So too should our worship reflect this theme, with each person coming forward to offer their gifts and talents before the Lord and each other.

A VISION OF HEALING

The Church at large is built like the tabernacle: God is the architect, and we carry out his instructions. "We are God's house of gemstones," writes James B. Jordan (*Through New Eyes,* 77). The Holy Spirit, the fire within our hearts, is a healer: healing the divisions between us as we engage in God's work of building the church. We long for relationships to be healed —between artists and pastors, among churches of different cultures, and within each of our souls.

Throughout the Old Testament, God's chosen people, Israel, experienced division: They endured schisms, division between tribes, and godless rulers. Christians today may empathize with the Israelites as we lament our divisions over theology and politics, endure further schisms, and mourn the fallout from church leaders who abuse their position and power over others. Since sin entered our world, creation has fallen and broken, yes; but that is not the way it was meant to be. Remember what God said after he had made the world: "And God saw everything that he had made, and behold, it was very good" (Genesis 1:31). In an imperfect world, God still wants to love us and bless us. He still wants to have a relationship with us. He wants time with us, and from the time we spend together with him, God wants to inspire us to create new works of art that might bless, inspire, and edify those around us.

As we carry God's people on our hearts, we carry their burdens, cares, and wounds before the Lord in intercessory prayer. We are called to be a people of peace and healing — a diverse, creative people that reflects the image of God, growing together as disciples of Christ.

A VISION OF HEAVEN

The tabernacle and its elements of worship were copies and shadows of their heavenly realities (Hebrews 8:5) — prophetic, artistic visions of the heavenly realm. Moses had to carry out his instructions with scrupulous obedience to point us to Jesus Christ, the great High Priest ministering in heaven (Hebrews 8:1–3). With this image in mind, we can imagine Christ wearing the real breastpiece as he carries us before the Father. In the words of James B. Jordan,

> ...the fact that the High Priest carried the gemstones on his heart means that we as God's gemstones are always next to the heart of Christ. We may feel like ugly gray rocks that have been cast aside; but we know in faith that God carries us on His heart, and we are of infinite value to Him. (*Through New Eyes*, 78)

If the passage above resonates with you today, allow me to reiterate that you are not an ugly gray rock. You are a precious gemstone. Imes declares,

> These gemstones daily remind Yahweh of his covenant commitment to the twelve tribes of Israel, and they ensure that each of the twelve has a place in his ministry. None can be marginalized or forgotten. They all belong. They are all Yahweh's treasured possession. On his head, Aaron wears a turban with a gold medallion tied with blue cords. The medallion reads "Holy, Belonging to Yahweh," just two words in Hebrew, *qodesh layahweh*. (*Bearing God's Name,* 73)

We carry you with us in our prayers and on our hearts. You are God's beloved.

One day, Christ will come again and make all things new. Until that time, let us create beautiful works of culture, filling the earth with music, paintings, and poetry. Let us proclaim the name of Christ with dance, drama and graphic design. Then, on that final day, may we rejoice and worship in united adoration as the Lamb takes the scroll. And may we join with all God's people in singing, "Worthy is the Lamb" (Revelation 5:12).

ARTIST'S BOOKSHELF

——

Here are several works that have inspired us as artists.

Michael Card, *A Sacred Sorrow: Reaching Out to God in the Lost Language of Lament* (Colorado Springs, CO: NavPress, 2005)

Andy Crouch, *Culture Making: Recovering Our Creative Calling* (Downers Grove, IL: IVP Books, 2008)

Makoto Fujimura, *Culture Care: Reconnecting with Beauty for Our Common Life* (Downers Grove, IL: IVP Books, 2017)

Makoto Fujimura, *Art and Faith: A Theology of Making* (New Haven, CT: Yale University Press, 2020)

John Paul II, "Letter to Artists" (Vatican: Easter 1999)

Madeleine L'Engle, *Walking on Water: Reflections on Faith and Art* (Colorado Springs, CO: Waterbrook Press, 1972)

Andrew Peterson, *Adorning the Dark: Thoughts on Community, Calling, and the Mystery of Making* (Nashville, TN: B&H Publishing Group, 2019)

W. David O. Taylor, *Glimpses of the New Creation: Worship and the Formative Power of the Arts* (Grand Rapids, MI: Eerdmans, 2019)

———. *For the Beauty of the Church: Casting a Vision for the Arts* (Grand Rapids, MI: Baker Books, 2010)

ABOUT THE CONTRIBUTORS

Kate Bluett | *The Colony, Texas*

Kate is a stay-at-home, homeschooling mom and writer from north Texas. She holds a BA and an MA from the University of Dallas, and she writes liturgical and devotional poetry and lyrics.

Rev. Dave Frincke | *Fort Wayne, Indiana*

Dave is an artist and a sixth-generation pastor who has a passion for pioneering new works and equipping people for ministry. He is the senior pastor of Heartland Church and the global movement leader for United Adoration. Dave lives on a farm with his wife, Bethany; their four children, Lily, Gideon, Elizabeth Joy, and Zadok; a menagerie of farm animals; and a peacock named Solomon. His recordings are *Priceless Treasure* (2008), a collection of hymns; *Songs and Praise for the Eucharist* (2012), with Heartland Church; *Rises from the Valleys* (2015), a selection of songs from the musical "Bend Us"; and *The First Dance* (2016), an instrumental album with Emma Woodward.

Hunter Lynch | *Vicksburg, Mississippi*

Hunter is married to Ellie and father to Laney and Emmalyn. He currently works as a worship and youth pastor at Highland Baptist in Vicksburg, Mississippi. An avid songwriter and writer, he enjoys leading song shares and working with Resound Worship's 12-Song Challenge. He is a graduate of Mississippi College (BA, Christian studies) and New Orleans Baptist Theological Seminary (MDiv).

Moses Kimani | *Nairobi, Kenya*

Moses (or "Kim," as he is affectionately known) is a disciple of Jesus with a passion for church music and organic discipleship. He is the Africa coordinator and Kenya regional leader for United Adoration. Moses, his wife Susan, and their two daughters live in the outskirts of the Kenyan capital, Nairobi.

REV. JACK KING | *Knoxville, Tennessee*

Jack is the rector of Church of the Apostles in Knoxville, Tennessee. He loves books — poetry, history, fiction, and biographies — and distance running. He enjoys playing guitar and hammered dulcimer, cooking for his wife Emily and friends, and following the Boston Red Sox. He holds a BA in history from Samford University (2000) and an MDiv from Duke Divinity School (2004).

KATHRYN KIRCHER | *Fort Wayne, Indiana*

Kathryn is a United Adoration staff member who loves to see God adored in the creativity of his people throughout the earth. Before joining United Adoration, she and her husband, Nick, served in Asia for more than a decade. Kathryn is the mother of five and grandmother of nine. Her new stay-at-home retreat guide, *Parables of the Eucalyptus*, includes a number of creative activities for connecting with God. It's available on Amazon in both Kindle and paperback formats.

ELISE MASSA | *Pittsburgh, Pennsylvania*

Elise serves as the Northeast regional leader for United Adoration and is also assistant director of music and worship arts at Church of the Ascension. Elise has a deep desire for all artists to be transformed by Jesus Christ and to find a home in his church. She believes that artists have a formative role in forging the church's identity and its witness to God's redemptive story for all people and creation. She has a particular vision for artists across disciplines to grow together and glean from one another in fellowship. She is inspired by the lives of St. Teresa of Ávila, Mahalia Jackson, Monet, Makoto Fujimura, John Donne, and Maya Angelou.

MELISSA AMBER McKINNEY | *Bellevue, Pennsylvania*

Melissa is a certified peer specialist, writer, and singer/songwriter who currently lives just north of Pittsburgh. She is the care team coordinator and sings and leads worship at her home church, Redeemer Anglican Church. You can find her album *Through Flood and Fire,* an EP of songs she's written through times of suffering and doubt, on Bandcamp.

CATHERINE MILLER | *Tallahassee, Florida*

Catherine is a singer-songwriter, writer, and pianist. Originally hailing from Miami, she moved to Tallahassee for college in 2005 and met Henry soon thereafter, marrying him after a courtship of three years. Three kids, two cats, a dog, and twelve years later, they enjoy working together, editing and songwriting as a couple. Catherine holds a BME from Florida State University and is working on her master's in worship studies at The Robert E. Webber Institute for Worship Studies in Jacksonville, Florida.

HENRY MILLER | *Tallahassee, Florida*

Henry is a poet, writer, and father of three rambunctious boys. He enjoys Nerf battles, Wendell Berry, and agri-ventures with his family.

NATHANAEL ORR | *Cwmbran, Wales, United Kingdom*

Nate is a singer-songwriter and is currently learning how best to serve career artists in their work. He trusts that God will teach and guide him to better understand the wounds in the art world and play a small part in helping to bring God's healing.

STEPHEN SLOSS | *Preston, England, United Kingdom*

Stephen is married to Linda and lives in the northwest of England near the city of Preston. He is a worship leader at St. Cuthbert's (Church of England) as well as a songwriter and social worker. He and Linda have three kids and six (rather fabulous) grandkids. Stephen leads Salvere, an organization helping people organize care and support.

RACHEL WILHELM | *Knoxville, Tennessee*

Rachel is minister of music and worship arts and a singer-songwriter at Apostles Anglican Church. She is also United States team leader for United Adoration, leading songwriting and worship-arts retreats for local churches and their artists. Her recordings are *A Kindling Glance* (EP, 2016), *Songs of Lament* (2017), and *Requiem* (2021).

ACKNOWLEDGMENTS

United Adoration is a movement of pastors and artists who want to see creativity revitalized in the local church.

To God our Father, the Son, and the Holy Spirit: thank you for creating us, saving us, and inspiring our work.

To Heartland Church, who hosts this ministry;

To Rachel Wilhelm and Catherine Miller, who poured their energy into pulling together this collection;

To Hunter Lynch, Kate Bluett, Henry Miller, and Kathryn Kircher, who worked diligently on editing the online blog that inspired this devotional;

To Dave Frincke, who always encourages us to listen to God and creates space for us to try new things;

To Barb Astrino and all of the intercessors around the world, who cover us in prayer;

To all who donated to United Adoration and made this publication possible;

To all the local churches, pastors, and artists around the world:

Thank you. Your work is beautiful.

Book packager and editorial consultant: *Garrett Brown, Merrifield Press*
Designer & cover illustrator: *Katherine Messenger*
Editor: *Kathy Shaibani*

The main text of this book is set in Hoefler Text & Titling, the headlines are set in Requiem, and the epigraphs are set in Ideal Sans; all were designed by Hoefler & Co. The floral motif, scattered throughout this book, as well as the rules at the opening of each section, the linear flourish after the byline, and the word "Amen" at the close of each section, are from the New Victorian Printshop suite of fonts and decorations made by the Walden Font Co.

CPSIA information can be obtained
at www.ICGtesting.com
Printed in the USA
JSHW031234101221
21046JS00001B/1

9 781737 927808